I Hate Being A Lawyer

I Hate Being A Lawyer

A Guide To Escaping The Nightmare

STEVE STALLMAN

I HATE BEING A LAYWER

Published by Blue Peg Publishing

If you have purchased the ebook version of this book, then please consider buying the print version if your family enjoys the ebook.

Contents

I Hate Being A Lawyer, Do You?

The world is full of jokes about hating lawyers. It's the profession that non-lawyers love to hate.

If you're a lawyer or you know one, you likely already know that.

But here's something you don't know.

For every joke about hating a lawyer there's a thousand working lawyers who despise their jobs even more than being the butt of those jokes.

There was a time when studying law was a ticket to career greatness and hefty bank accounts. But that is history, according to a job satisfaction study conducted by the American Bar Foundation.

Today's reality is that the average lawyer is even more disenchanted with the legal profession than those who make up sarcastic jokes about it.

Only one in four lawyers says they would recommend being a lawyer to someone else. Most describe themselves as "deeply unhappy."

Across the planet there is a whole "I hate being a lawyer" movement. Young, well-educated men and women are looking to escape what they perceive as a nightmare of a career.

That is a lot of unhappy people, because there are a lot of lawyers on this planet. Israel has one lawyer for every 170 people. The United States has one for every 265 Americans. Brazil has one lawyer for every 326 people.

There are more than 1.4 million lawyers in the United States alone, and more than one million in India.

Discontent is prevalent in the profession. Pundits call it a "crisis of morale."

Yale Professor Dean Kronman, in an article called "Lawyers and Their Discontents" by John P. Heinz, defined it as "the product of growing doubts about the capacity of a lawyer's life to offer fulfillment to the person who takes it up. Disguised by the material well-being of lawyers, it is a spiritual crisis that strikes at the heart of their professional pride."

A study conducted by the California Bar Journal concluded that 75 per cent of lawyers surveyed did not want their children to become lawyers.

A university study in North Carolina revealed that 11 percent of their state attorneys considered taking their own lives at least once a month.

The media spotlight has turned glaringly on the gaping hole between expectations and returns in the legal profession. A recent headline in the *Los Angeles Times* proclaims: "Miserable With The Legal Life: More And More Lawyers Hate Their Jobs, Surveys Find."

The Denver Business Journal ran an article headlined: "Running From The Law: Attorneys After Happiness Find It In Other Jobs."

One lawyer's blog noted that the television hit "Harry's Law" is right on point, especially in the episode where Prosecutor Puck talks about how he is a ball of nerves and lost all his hair because of his job.

Although it is difficult to pinpoint statistically, estimates suggest that in the United States alone, 30,000 lawyers a year leave the profession.

In an article entitled "Choose Living Over Lawyering," published June 30, 2011, former lawyer turned stand-up comic Alex Barnett talks at length about his growing disillusionment with his profession.

"Ultimately, any small moments of satisfaction and joy you can find in a job well done will disappear and you will find yourself staring up from the bottom of the abyss," he concludes. "This feeling is so pervasive amongst lawyers that bar associations across the country have set up suicide hotlines. When you call, they say "What took you so long?"

"If you're smart (smarter than me), this is when you realize it's time to make a change," he adds.

Barnett says he finally figured out that living a life of fear is no life at all.

"Let go of the safety bar," he urges fellow lawyers who have become disenchanted. "Figure out what you really want ----NOW!"

For him the road to a new life was a second career as a stand-up comic.

"I had to go back to square one," he confessed. "I had been a partner in a law firm, 14 years of private practice under my belt, and I went back to the beginning."

As tough as his new life is, he prefers it to his old one.

"It's the satisfaction that I don't have to ruin yet another weekend slaving away over a brief that no one will read. It's the satisfaction of knowing I'm doing something I really want to do, not something that I think other people think I should be doing. It's the satisfaction of not having to give free legal advice to crazy relatives and friends of friends who want to know what to do now that their landlord found out they have a collection of scorpions, tarantulas and poisonous snakes."

At the "lifeatthebar.com" blog, Julie A. Fleming wrote a post called "I Hate Being A Lawyer." When you say that, she asked, "what does it mean to you to be a lawyer? How do you interpret that identity, and what do you dislike about it?

"The bottom line, of course, is that making the statement 'I hate being a lawyer' calls for some kind of action. Maybe the action is a job/career change, or maybe it's analysis to identify what changes would negate that statement (partly or completely) and making those changes."

That's the essence of what this book is about. If you are a lawyer, and you hate it, how DO you escape the nightmare? Can you regroup and reinvent yourself in some other aspect of the legal profession?

Or should you leave it completely? What kind of options do you have with legal training behind you?

What steps can you take to prepare your exit strategy and build your new life while you still get income from your old?

Where do you look for work that really matters? Should you look for another job or go out on a limb and start your own business?

Or maybe happiness comes with an even bigger change for you. You may decide after a lot of soul-searching to embrace a new code of voluntary simplicity and completely change your life to make it better.

Walking away from a profession you hate takes courage, as does embracing a new lifestyle of changing jobs or even scaling down and spending less. But overall, you may find a new wealth in a world of freedom and independence.

Peter Shankman, owner of the HARO newsletter and website, in his article called "How to Jailbreak Your Life So You Can Live the Way You Want," says there are six excuses people give for not doing what they really want to do.

One is that you don't have the money, the second is that you have a paying job and a family and can't afford to leave it, the third is that you think your friends would never understand, the fourth is that your spouse and children would suffer, the fifth is that you're scared to lose your direct deposit salary, and the sixth is that you don't have the time to plan and make a lifestyle change.

Do some or all of these apply to you?

Shankman's point is that all of these hesitations are just blockades that you can move easily if you really want to change your life. You likely don't need as much money as you think you do to be happy. While it's true you have to think of your family's needs, you don't have to quit cold turkey to start the process of making significant changes in your life.

Your friends, your true friends, want to see you happy, and if that means you not being a lawyer, they don't really care. If they can't accept that you need to make changes to be happy, change your friends. It is really that simple.

The fear of losing your direct deposit salary is a real one and it would be foolhardy to diminish it. But your fear can also be used to push you to your new goal. It will ensure that you prepare yourself for your new life so you have a reasonable chance of a soft landing when you jump into it.

Are you ready to start on the journey to work and life happiness? If you hate being a lawyer, you have options galore and this book will open your mind to thinking about them.

You can start living your dreams and escaping your nightmare. We will show you how.

Chapter 2

How Did Your Dream Become A Nightmare?

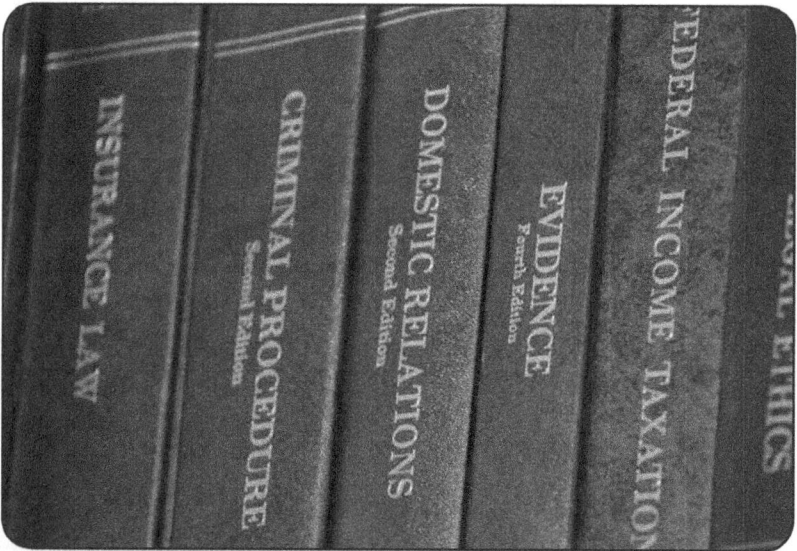

You likely still remember the pride on your Mom and Dad's faces when you graduated from law school. To a generation of parents who struggled to get most of their formal training on the job, to see their offspring walk out with a law parchment is fulfillment of their dream that you will have a better, more comfortable life than they did.

In some instances, when one of your parents had or has a fulfilling law career, there is an additional beam of pride that speaks of the satisfaction of seeing you following in their footsteps. In their minds, the cycle of prosperity becomes complete and their job has been well and truly done.

You and they are all hopeful when it starts that you are headed for a dream job with great money, status and promotion opportunities.

There are a lot of things nobody talks about, however.

One of them is charting every single work task you complete in terms of time spent on it, an endless time-tracking routine that needs to be meticulous and justifiable not only to clients (why is it so much?) but to bosses and senior partners (why is it so little?).

Another is the endless paperwork. Legal documentation is complex, so in the beginning, it is challenging and arduous and stressful. In the end it is challenging and arduous and increasingly boring, which in turn is still stressful.

People think there is glamour in your profession. They watch courtroom dramas on the movie screens and see clever lawyers out-debating other clever lawyers and it all seems exciting and edgy. What they don't see and what you know is that when you are a litigating lawyer, you rarely get any courtroom drama.

What you really get is hours and hours of preparing documents and renews, and then settling ultimately before things get to the courtroom stge.

But there's still the money and the thoughts of the life it can allow you to lead. Many a man and woman in today's world steadies their shoulders and endures a less than satisfying work environment to earn sufficient money to allow them to lead the life they yearn for when they are outside of the office.

You are willing to settle for that. Your income is solid and growing. So you tell yourself and your family that if you just endure the day to day dissatisfaction, it will be bearable when you all escape for the weekend to the cottage on the lake.

You see yourself sailing into sunsets, taking dream vacations, skiing in the Alps, jogging on the endless beaches, and it's not so bad after all. You can do it.

Trouble is, every time you book a weekend off, some client calls in a panic because he needs to buy a company and have his bids ready for Monday morning, and he needs you right now, to get started and spend all weekend working...again.

The crises are all different. But they are all the same in that you find yourself jumping to serve somebody else's needs at the expense of your own.

It doesn't take too many years before that price becomes too high.

While all of this is happening, deep inside the uneasy feeling that what you do doesn't really matter like you thought it would has taken root and starts to grow.

From watching television dramas, your original dream when you walked out of law school was all about helping society's victims, those who are wronged and cannot fight for justice for themselves.

Enter the hero lawyer. You can see clearly how the aggrieved tenant can acquire justice from the greedy landlord. You can fight for a fair settlement for the aggrieved spouse left with scarcely enough cash for groceries. You can help the injured win money for their hospital bills, the person unjustly accused with a crime to prove his innocence, and the downtrodden to rise again and triumph.

Your nightmare is that most of your clients are wallowing in pain and greed, and no matter what you do, it won't be enough to earn that grateful smile and earnest handshake. Instead, they will bitterly challenge your bill and perhaps not even pay it at all.

You can find yourself fighting for justice for people who are clearly schemers and dealers trying to take advantage of the justice system. You find yourself trying to enjoy a beer at the local watering hole but instead being hit up for free advice by some drunk whose spouse has finally packed up and left.

There is little solace in the camaraderie of other lawyers. They are competitive by nature, and showing empathy or understanding is generally seen as a sign of weakness. If you are unhappy, for every colleague who taps you on the shoulder and manages an insincere moment of concern, there is another noting that you should be easier to beat now if your morale is down.

You want to do work that really matters, but you realize someday that your real legacy is just going to be an archive full of dusty documents that will never see the light of day.

Then there is the psychological challenge of trying to deliver certainty in a profession that is being reinterpreted every day by judges and arbiters. So you research and you write, always trying to reach that certainty, yet always aware that the target is moving.

All of these thoughts and actions operate under a cloak of urgency. In the law business, everything is on deadline and that deadline was yesterday. At first you just try to catch up, but a few years into it, you realize there is no day that you feel you are ahead of the clock. Then some little thing happens in your own life and you suddenly realize that the effect of racing to the finish line has made you extremely aggressive and impatient.

If you have to live your life like you a flying a jet plane full throttle into the fog, then you have little empathy for others who want to take their time and live life within time, not against it.

You know there are exceptions to this bleakness, and you want to be in that part of the career world. Sometimes you can manage that, but when you can't, you are suddenly hit with the sobering, nagging reality: you have to get out.

It doesn't get any easier after you come to that conclusion.

Almost immediately after you open your mental shutter a crack to let the light of freedom in, you quickly close it again, washed away in a tsunami of guilt.

Your degree alone cost a small fortune, and you and others made serious sacrifices that cannot be taken lightly. Then there's the time of your life, often measured in years and even decades, that you invested in this career to build up what appears to others to be "success."

If your whole family has gotten use to living on a certain standard of income, there's also the understanding that your decision to change will impact many more people than yourself. Can you ask more of your spouse and children?

You overspend to buy them the things that you can't give them yourself, mostly your time. You overspend to give yourself the things you can't accomplish with your work: the sense of excitement and fulfillment we all yearn for.

But the firmer you plant your feet behind your desk, the harder it becomes to push back the chair and walk away. And the more you spend, the more the debt noose tightens around your white-collared neck and you wonder if you will ever escape or just dangle there in some kind of limbo until you die or retire.

You deserve a better life.

Everybody does.

The day you finally accept that nobody needs to be trapped forever doing the work they originally trained for is the day you start to make positive change in your life.

The world is full of people who have adapted some skills to do other skills. The banks are full of money earned by people who started down one road and recalculated to a more successful, fulfilling path to riches.

If you once thought you wanted to be a lawyer, but you hate it now, you've taken a solid first step in accepting your new reality.

All that remains is to figure out how to make use of your considerable skills in new ways and start the long climb up to a new perspective on life as it is meant to be lived.

Chapter 3

Why Breaking Up With The Law Firm Is So Hard To Do

Even when lawyers hate their work, the option of just leaving rarely seems viable.

The high-achieving lawyer who was drawn to the challenges of the profession in the first place is not a person who wants to feel like he or she can't do something.

Lawyers are just not wired to quit.

So instead of considering your future path as an "opting out" consider it a new stage in the process of negotiating a better life.

You wouldn't walk away from a business merger for your client with the feeling you were leaving money on the table. You wouldn't recommend to a client that they settle when you sensed there was still something more to gain. You wouldn't advise your client in the midst of divorce settlement negotiations to leave a lucrative life for one of poverty.

So there's no need to negotiate a bad deal for you.

You know in your heart you want to make a major life change. But in our culture, we have the unfortunate concept that "change" in the sense of stepping out of a rat race means "downsizing" or having something less.

In instance after instance we find that it really means negotiating something more: a richer, fuller and more rewarding life.

Treat yourself like your best, most valuable client. Now is the time to plan your strategy for how you will negotiate the best possible new life for yourself.

Take solace from the fact that you will not be the first or the most famous lawyer to walk away from your profession and branch out to follow a life that holds more promise of fulfilment.

Likely the most famous lawyer to re-invent himself away from his practice was American John Grisham, one of only three authors to sell two million copies on a first printing (the others were Tom Clancy and J. K. Rowling).

The ring of authenticity that makes Grisham's legal thrillers so enticing stems largely from the reality that he practiced criminal law for about a decade.

In fact, he only walked away to his real love of writing after the success of his second book, *The Firm,* when he had established sufficient financial success to make a seamless life transition.

Interestingly enough, in his search to do creative work that mattered, he never gave up his interest in law, only his day-to-day practice of it.

He returned to his practice briefly in 1996 to fight for the family of a railroad worker who was killed on the job.

His official site states that: "He was honoring a commitment made before he had retired from the law to become a full-time writer. Grisham successfully argued his clients' case, earning them a jury award of $683,000 U.S. – the biggest verdict of his career."

Grisham wasn't the only ex-lawyer to win the world's attention when he re-invented himself as something else.

The great musical composer Cole Porter starting his working life with an unsuccessful Harvard law career. The man who paid all his bills, his grandfather J.O. Cole, disapproved of men choosing careers in the arts and tried hard to convince Cole to be a lawyer.

But Cole wasn't happy with the law as a profession. All he ever wanted to do was write music, and lawyers will still find it somewhat ironic that one of Porter's first big hits was "Don't Fence Me In."

His many musicals and hits like "Let's Do It (Let's Fall in Love)" and "Night and Day" live on long after the world has forgotten any legal briefs he might have written.

Russian composer Peter Tchaikovsky, whose "Nutcracker Suite" charms the world as it is replayed every Christmas season, started life as a lawyer. Cuban revolutionary Fidel Castro, who became first Prime Minister and then President of his country, was a lawyer, graduating from the University of Havana.

United States President Barack Obama is a former lawyer, as was Bill Clinton, Thomas Jefferson, Abraham Lincoln and a host of other ex-presidents. Frances Scott Key, the man who wrote the moving and memorable American national anthem "The Star-Spangled Banner," was also a lawyer who maintained a duo career as a poet. It was Key who also successfully pushed the American government to adopt "In God We Trust" as the nation's motto.

More than two thirds of Canada's prime ministers since Confederation have been lawyers and many of the United

Kingdom's most distinguished Prime Ministers, such as Disraeli and Atlee, were also lawyers.

The list of the one-time lawyers turned full-time creative star seems endless. Add to it Martin Stone, originator of television's *Howdy Doody*, Martin Perelmuter, co-founder of Speaker's Spotlight that represents more than 600 speakers including Justin Trudeau and Pamela Walin in Canada, and Simon Broomer, founder and director of CareerBalance, a career planning and job search company.

Where do you fit on this list?

If you are still trying to find the strength to change your current life to a future life that fulfills you, don't make the mistake of thinking that your legal training and experience has been a waste of time. In fact, it will turn into a great asset as you start your search for reinvention.

A *Wall Street Journal report* entitled "Want to Leave the Law? Ex-lawyer Explains the Upside" (Feb. 2, 2010) tells the story of Cari Sommer who practiced law for seven years before she founded Urban Interns, a website that connects small business owners with job hunters seeking part-time work. She makes a point of expressing how valuable her law background is to her new career.

"In the broadest terms, practicing law is about analyzing facts, solving problems, advocating a position, and communicating with clients and adversaries," she says. "I use these skills every day in my work as an entrepreneur."

What rings consistently through the interviews with lawyers who left their legal profession for other career paths is to do serious research before you walk away from your practice.

Those who have been successful with their transition tell how they had to curb the urge to act on impulse because of a disagreeable client or boss. Instead, they used such situations as a catalyst for serious research and a well-reasoned plan of action for renewing themselves.

Keep your job while you explore your options, they urge.

But don't just research job options and how you can transfer your skills to new careers. Research yourself and what you really want out of life.

Ask yourself how your time in your legal career has impacted you as a person. Do the long hours mean you have grown uncomfortably out of shape? Do you have money, but no time, to go to the gym or take up an active copy?

How are you handling stress? Are you still thinking about your job long after you should have transferred your thoughts to other aspects of your home life? Are you tense and irritable? Is your overall health hurting because of your job?

Re-examine why you entered law as your professional originally, and consider if those reasons or goals are still valid? Were you pushed into it, or did you select it or was it the best choice because you had no idea what you really wanted to do?

Did you want to be a lawyer from the beginning and now wonder what went horribly wrong?

Have you become the kind of lawyer that you imagined you would be?

Do you still have moments of passion for what you do, or are you totally disillusioned and bored? Do you feel that you have to work much harder than others, and that you get the worst cases?

Are you working in fear that you will be fired at any moment?

These are all questions that will pop into your head once you start seriously questioning your career choice.

What you may not consider, however, is how much of your identity is wrapped up in being a lawyer? When you are introduced to someone and they ask what you do, how does it feel to tell them you are a lawyer? Does it feel good? Or is it an uncomfortable truth you would rather avoid?

How else could you describe yourself? Could you say "I'm a musician, but I practice law to pay my bills." Is your "elevator speech" one dimensional, or are there many facets to your self-description?

Before you move into new fields, think about how you would like to describe yourself.

Opening your mind to considerations of where you really are and where you would rather be is the beginning of a long journey to an enhanced life and self-fulfillment.

But before you get there, there are always some uncomfortable realities to be faced.

If you are like most lawyers, debt is one of them.

Chapter 4

Disengaging Yourself Out Of The Debt Trap

When you feel enslaved to your legal profession but can't leave it, chances are the toughest, biggest chain holding you to your desk is debt.

The borrowing usually starts during university and it continues and escalates as the lawyer lifestyle encourages you to spend to keep up appearances and keep up with the neighbours.

The average student in the United States, for example, leaves university with their degree in one hand and a debt of about $25,000 in the other. Young law students usually owe even more. Even a mention that you are studying law is sufficient to get you more money than you can really afford to borrow.

Then you buy a car, and join the 70 percent of people buying cars who need to take out loans to pay for them. And then comes the credit cards and the high balances that more than 46 per cent of all Americans carry over month to month.

You buy a house much bigger than you can afford even before you make partner in the firm, because the mortgage firm agrees that your prospects are very bright indeed.

The people in that neighbourhood all send their children to private school, so you can't have yours not going there, can you? And so the tuition treadmill starts again.

Then come the toys to cope with the boredom of doing what you do. The boat, the fast cars, the house at the seashore or in the mountains or in some exotic get-away that you never really have time to enjoy.

Before you can quit being a lawyer, you need a strategy to get your debt under control.

Even in the worst case scenario, you should be able to escape your consumer debt within 18-24 months if you really put your mind to it. You may end up taking extra work, piling up the overtime.

If you know it's going to take you longer than that, you need to sell something that is being debt-financed, like your car or your boat or your vacation home.

You also need to observe a moratorium on spending for anything but essentials, starting now.

This is important because when you start to examine options for getting out of the legal profession, one of them may be purchasing a business, whether a franchise or an independent operation.

What you don't want to do is finance your freedom with more debt until you find you are still a slave, that all you have done is sold yourself to a new owner.

Remember that debt is what chains you and everyone else to living lives you don't want. We may blame a long list of other things, and some of them are true, but 10 to one if you really look at yourself in the mirror and ask why you continue to do work you hate, the answer that comes back loud and clear is "debt."

You have no choice. Until you realize that you do.

As part of your debt reduction strategy, make sure that you set up a modest emergency fund for unscheduled car maintenance or leaking roofs or broken windows.

When you start paying off your credit cards, instead of being discouraged at the enormity of the task, break your challenge into a number of small, achievable milestones. Then have small victory celebrations as each balance is finally paid off.

There are many strategies for dropping your credit card balances: we tend to favour trying to wipe out the card with the lowest debt load and then moving on. This may not be the most logical process, but it is definitely the tried and true way that most people embrace for success.

One of the reasons is that this gives you a sense of accomplishment well before the end of your journey. These feelings of accomplishment are essential to keep your spirits up as you slowly step closer to the life to which you aspire.

When you find yourself wavering, close your eyes and picture yourself finally free from both the job you dislike and the debt that keeps you there. It will be your most powerful incentive and will give you the courage to say no when you have to.

With each debt pay-off, spend extra time putting your plan together to start your new life. The surge of energy that comes with paying off each card will invigorate you and encourage you to stay the course until you reach your debt-free destination.

Look around you at this time as you plan to leave your old life and ask what else do you not want to carry to your new life?

For example, do you really love to golf, or is it something you just do because you feel you have to? Are the new clubs and cart really going to be essential in your new profession, whatever that may be?

Is that time-share vacation plan ever going to pay for itself, or would you be better off selling it and saving your funds to take a vacation to a part of the world that doesn't fit in somebody else's plan?

Here is a checklist of six essential steps to consider when you devise your getting-out-of-debt plan:

Don't go into more debt. From this point forward, use cash for all your purchases and give family members, if it is your responsibility to support them, their allotted allowances in cash with no more coming until the following month.

Figure out your monthly and yearly budget. We know, budget is a bad word, but so is "despise" when it comes to what you do for a living. Make sure that the final balance of your budget means that you will spend considerably less than you earn.

While you are creating your budget, take stock of all your liabilities. If you are going to come clean, you have to know how deeply your debt is buried. Create a spreadsheet and outline monthly payments, interest accumulation, and balances, and update it every single month.

As soon as your debt payoff is completed, keep to the same schedule of handling your money, only now start to put 60 percent into savings and live on the remaining 40 percent.

Aim to spend the rest of your life with one credit card with a low limit, and allow yourself only one loan at any given time (for the purchase of a car, for example). This loan should never exceed 25 percent of your income.

Don't give up just because this is one of the hardest things you will ever do in life. It hurts now, but if you do this right now, it will never hurt you again.

Chapter 5

How To Plan Your Exit Strategy

Jumping off a ledge without a parachute rarely ends well. You may feel depressed and frustrated and even resentful that life has made you a lawyer, but you could feel worse. Unemployed, hungry and homeless is worse.

What you need before you leave your lawyer's desk is a parachute which will come disguised as a solid plan for assessing how the skills you have acquired can be applied to other things in life to provide you with a comfortable income and more enjoyable lifestyle.

It is highly advisable to do all your planning and even take several steps in the direction of change from the desk where you currently work. Whether your dream ends with you embracing entrepreneurship, backpacking in Tibet, lecturing in a college, or growing potatoes organically in a nearby countryside, you will find it easier to dream and plan with the security of your regular paycheque coming in.

Invest in a notebook or a technological device that allows you to record thoughts and research when you see or hear something with future potential, allowing you to store it up and sift through it on weekends.

Planning your exit strategy is a lot about researching and gathering intelligence as you explore your many options, weighing pros and cons about your reinvention strategy, and then ultimately setting a goal and moving steadfastly in that direction.

It may seem strange that to gain your freedom you must first work harder than ever, partly to eliminate your debt and secondly to plan your future, but it is the formula for loosening those legal shackles.

You are already well on your way to creating a solid exit strategy. You set two strategic goals and are now making a plan to achieve them. You set debt reduction as a first goal, and career change as a second.

Now let us consider the options for applying the skills you have invested time, energy and considerable money in acquiring.

By the nature of what you do as a lawyer, you can read, write and do research at a level far superior to the average person. Those skills are the stock and trade of your business skills.

You can think logically, have great analytical skills, and can strategize through an intricate pattern to reach a desired conclusion.

You can plan and plot and pursue a desired goal with incredible focus and vision. Plus, you know which steps are legal and which are illegal and the gray edges of both worlds.

All of these natural skills that you likely take for granted immediately present options for you. You could be a writer of legal thrillers or legal textbooks or legal blogs. You could teach law, or you could be a legal advisor on a television or radio show or write a legal advice column for a newspaper.

You could write how-to books about how to handle some of life's legal challenges, like how to get a divorce, how to write a will, how to purchase property and how to arrange a pre-nuptial agreement. You could write such books and then sell them as eBooks online with a supporting program of webinars.

You could teach either at a university or community college level. You might have to go back for a little additional training, but it will be nothing compared to the years you invested in the study of law.

You could teach the rudiments of corporate and industrial law to business students; you could teach the basics of registering and establishing a business for aspiring entrepreneurs through seminars at economic development agencies.

You could research and write white papers on all manner of subjects, some of a legal nature and some not. You could analyze data for a marketing research firm or an intelligence agency.

You could leave criminal or corporate law and become a labour negotiator. You could leave industrial relations law and become an expert in tax law and develop books, seminars and courses around that new area of expertise.

But here's the amazing thing about your options.

Even if there is absolutely nothing you want to do that touches the world of law, lawyers and legalities, you still have your reading, writing, researching, and analytical skills to take with you.

You could leave law and go into the arts, returning to university to study psychology or theology or media and culture. You may want to try your hand at creative writing, composing and performing music, creating art or sculpture or baking amazing cakes.

Many ex-lawyers, particularly those practicing criminal law, have found that it wasn't so much the routine of their jobs that bothered them after several years; it was the routine of their clients. So many declare they will reform after a scrap with the law, but end up keeping you on their speed dial because reform is easy to say, hard to do.

In the world of creative arts and literature, disillusioned lawyers can often find true happiness and wealth. If you still can't totally escape your old world, you can muster your writing skills to draw others to the downside of your legal career. You can create a popular website to show both the ups and downs of your past profession, like www. bitterlawyer.com or www.lawyermeltdown.com.

You could go into business. Your legal skills and powers of analyzing information quickly and accurately will serve you in good stead. Become a health care lawyer, start a florist business, or set up a practice to support non-profit agencies doing real work that matters.

You could become a property developer or home builder.

Remember that one of the most common complaints of lawyers when they become severely disillusioned is that they have nothing to show for their work except boxes and boxes of documents that will likely never again see the light of day.

It might be fun to contemplate pointing to a neighbourhood or condo development that you planned and created. You might enjoy the thrill of driving by your own apartment building or strip mall or professional building full of doctors and therapists and other healing professions. Tackling such projects will be easier when you bring your legal background with you.

The ways that lawyers are reinventing themselves is well chronicled. The U.S. News and World Report ran an article called "Alternative Career Options for Lawyers" that elicited wide response. In it, they chronicled the success stories of many former lawyers who had built new lives incorporating their own skills. For example, Tonya Fitzpatrick, a former high powered lawyer who had worked for the Department of Homeland Security, told how she is now the co-host, with her husband, of a radio show called World Footprints, and creator of a media company with a travel focus.

Ellen Covner, a former health care lawyer, started a landscaping business outside of Philadelphia, U.S. She found it a great way to use her analytical skills and help her clients plan beautiful properties suited to their personalities.

If you want to exit the practice of law, you can also consider public speaking, coaching or counselling, or working as a lobbyist or advocate for a cause you believe in.

In a popular book called "This Is Not The Career I Ordered," author Caroline Dowd-Higgins says lawyers tend to have excellent written and verbal communication skills, and these are highly valuable and transferable skills. She suggests that there are many things people can do with a law degree, and many of them have nothing at all to do with being a lawyer.

According to Heather Krasna, author of "Jobs That Matter: Finding A Fulfilling Career in Public Service," law is a valuable degree to have, even if you don't want to use it anymore.

Still searching for more ideas of what you could do when you leave law? There's always being a law librarian, an insurance agent selling products exclusively to lawyers, a legal videographer (covering accident scenes, etc.), a head-hunter for legal firms or a service provider to legal firms (computer systems and software), management consulting, or an agent for athletes or entertainers.

You could become a business evaluation expert, a director of ethics for a hospital, university or government agency, a risk manager for an insurance agency, a political campaign manager, a grant proposal writer, or even a legal counsel working exclusively with other lawyers.

The road clearly leads in more directions than simply "in" or "out." Take your time and think about which option is most appealing to you. In the coming chapters, we'll explore these options in more detail.

Chapter 6

Making Your Move
But Staying In
The Legal Profession

Allison C. Shields, a practicing lawyer whose company Legalease Consulting Inc. works to prevent the defection of good lawyers from the profession and to help lawyers rediscover their reason for going into the law in the first place, says the process of re-igniting your passion both inside and outside of your law practice ends up increasing your bottom line.

Shields, who writes regular articles on her website www. lawyermeltdown.com , says she started to write while she was going through her own meltdown.

She wanted to find a way to tell lawyers that they didn't have to kill themselves and be miserable to be "successful." Her solution was to amass lots of free information and links to resources that helped her, and then pass them on to others who are trying to escape the never-ending trap of work, work and more work.

If your hatred or disillusionment is not for the entire legal profession, but rather for the way you have to work within it, it makes sense to follow Shields' example and start amassing research and information now on how you can change your career, but still stay in the business that originally attracted you.

There's an excellent chance that you can "escape" to a new freedom of work simply by transferring to another branch of the business.

How do you know if your relationship with your legal career is worth saving?

You start by asking yourself all the same questions you would consider if you wanted to leave a bad marriage or an untenable living situation. What is it about your legal career that is making you unhappy? Is it your boss, your co-workers, the actual work you do, or just some aspect of the work you do? Think about what it is that makes you most unhappy in your workplace. Try to pinpoint it as precisely as possible. How much of your work day is spent doing the tasks that you don't like at all?

What parts of your current career would you actually miss if you just walked away from it today? Are there tasks in your daily and weekly routine that you enjoy or that give you satisfaction? Think about these.

Take the time to sit quietly and make some notes about your likes and dislikes in your career. Your lists will be crucial in helping you decide whether you want to throw it all away and move to a completely new field, or whether you want to initiate serious changes but still find a way to work within the legal business.

If your self-analysis reveals that you are unhappy in almost every aspect of your career as a lawyer, then take the steps now to get out and start something news. Staying out of habit or debt or fear of change will slowly suck the life right out of you.

According to career coaches Olga Artman, Celia Paul and Stephen Rosen, the most common causes of distaste for the legal profession among solo practitioners can be itemized.

In an article called "Careers Are Like Marriages: Find The One You Want or Fix The One You Have," they cite them as lack of having vision for the practice, not knowing where to find clients, fears of inadequacy, poor time management, the hours spent away from loved ones, the pressure of generating new clients, the stress of carrying sole responsibility for generating income, and losing interest in the job.

Supposing that after your self-analysis, you decide that you want to make a career move, but stay within the legal profession, what are your options?

If you don't like criminal or corporate law, for example, you might reawaken your passion for the profession by switching over to intellectual property law.

The growing use of the Internet has prompted a need for a whole new crop of lawyers who understand cyber worlds and how property still needs to be controlled and protected within them.

With an aging world population, the fertile ground of estate planning is becoming more and more in demand. Helping decent people find the ways and means to set up worthwhile legacies for charitable organizations or to channel their money to make a better life for their children and grandchildren is interesting and often worthwhile work. In the same vein, there is a growing field in elder law as the baby boomer clearly illustrates theirs is not the generation to shuffle off quietly to a rocking chair.

Still another growing specialty is education law, working with universities and public and private schools. Many of the larger education facilities actually have lawyers on staff, while a decent living could be made among the smaller ones with consulting services.

In the wake of a global recession, the field of employment law and bankruptcy law has also been growing rapidly. Helping people to get the best possible deals in difficult times is challenging but also rewarding work.

Climate change, disposal of hazardous products, and personal and corporate responsibility for our planet have all contributed to a growing demand for lawyers specializing in environmental law. Other specialties include immigration law and health care law.

Being a lawyer doesn't have to mean living a big life in a big city either. All across North America and Europe and Asian, there are hundreds of thousands of rural communities where a one-person practice brings a steady and diverse stream of demands for services. One day you may be assisting a rancher to buy cattle, another day you might be helping the local dairy negotiate an overseas sale, and later that day, you might need to help a person who has lost his job unfairly.

It is these small practices that allow the lawyer to reconnect with the pulse of ordinary life and play an essential role in the well-being of the community. While the remuneration may be less than a partnership in a big-city firm, so are the living expenses and demands on your time. Remember what a weekend used to feel like? You could get to experience that again.

Other lawyers find ways to divide their careers into segments that they enjoy. For example, you could practice corporate law during the day, but one night a week teach a legal class at a community college. If you are hoping down the line to eventually leave the corporate practice and delve into the world of writing law textbooks and seminars, this experience will be invaluable to start you in the right direction.

Change is difficult. We are all afraid of jumping out of the frying pan and into the fire. We fear that when we make a change, we might just make things worse, and even more disconcerting, find that we make precisely the same mistakes again.

It helps to remember that if you find the courage to change once, you can find it again. Dig deep within yourself for the courage to step outside your comfort zone and try something new. Be confident that if it doesn't end up as you hope, you now know the most important thing: that you can change, and you will change again.

Chapter 7

Turn Your Researching and Writing Skills Into A Career

Former Boston lawyer David E. Kelley, by his own admission, tends to be "a little grand in terms of storytelling.

"I've never been limited by anybody's sense of reality," he admits.

41

So he turned some of the scenes he witnessed as a lawyer into a screenplay, ramped it up with his fertile imagination, and moved to Hollywood to seek a new life.

The Maine native, now 56, ended up living the great American dream. He switched careers to become a successful producer, made millions and married movie star Michelle Pfeiffer.

He became the first producer ever to win Emmy and Golden Globe Awards in both the Outstanding/Best Drama Series (*The Practice, 1997*) and Outstanding/Best Comedy Series (*Ally McBeal, 1997*) categories in the same year (1999).

He created winning show after winning show. The most Kelley-created shows to be on at once were five during the 1999-2000 television season: *Chicago Hope* (1994) on CBS, *The Practice* (1997) and *Snoops* (1999) on ABC, and *Ally McBeal* (1997) and *Ally* (1999) on Fox.

Kelley was an associate at Fine & Ambrogne in 1983 when he wrote his first film script based on some of his legal experience. With the help of a family friend, he got the script optioned and acquired an agent three years later. The next year the script was produced as a film called *From The Hip* starring Judd Nelson, Elizabeth Perkins and John Hurt.

It was a firm start to a career different from the daily practice of law, but it was also just the tip of the iceberg. TV producers Steven Bochco and Terry Louise Fisher (who had created the police drama *Hill Street Blues*) were planning a new series called *L.A. Law* and they were looking for writers with a legal background. They invited Kelley to Los Angeles to discuss writing one single script for the show.

Kelley ended up being story editor for the show and ultimately, after Terry Fisher left, the supervising producer and then, after Bochco left, as executive producer.

He continued to branch out and create new shows and new scripts, becoming one of Hollywood's most sought after talents.

For every disillusioned unhappy lawyer with a half-written legal script in their desk drawer, he continues to serve as an inspiration that there is life outside of the law practice.

So does Scott Turow, the American author and lawyer whose eight fiction and two nonfiction books have been translated into more than 20 languages and sold more than 25 million copies.

Movies have been based on many of his books.

The Chicago native and Harvard Law School graduate earned his Juris Doctor (J.D.) degree in 1978 and became an Assistant United States Attorney in Chicago, a post he held until 1986.

During that time he prosecuted several high-profile corruption cases.

He left the U.S. Attorney's office to become a novelist, and his legal thrillers like "The Burden of Proof", "Presumed Innocent", "Pleading Guilty" and "Personal Injuries" all became bestsellers.

Time Magazine christened him the "Bard of the Litigious Age" when they featured him on their June 11, 1990 cover.

And although Turow's career took him far from his day-to-day law practice, he is still a partner of the Chicago law firm of Sonnenschein Nath & Rosenthal. He works pro bono in most of his cases, including a 1995 case where he achieved the release of Alejandro Hernandez, who spent 11 years on Death Row for a murder he did not commit.

While Kelley and Turow are cases of extreme good fortune following their change from a legal career, there are other less spectacular stories of former lawyers finding fulfilling lives by turning their writing and researching skills towards more creative pursuits.

Take the case of Canadian freelance writer Valerie Mutton who writes magazine features and murder mystery storylines for CSI Miami and CSI Las Vegas board games.

After 15 years of practising family and criminal law with a partner in Bowmanville, near Toronto, Ontario, she writes that she started feeling "like I wanted something different in my life.

"Practicing law wasn't fun anymore," she says.

Her work now appears in such magazines as *More, Oxygen* and *Today's Parent*. But she hasn't released all ties with her old profession.

Instead, she uses her training to be able to write about legal issues for the *National* and *The Lawyer's Weekly*. She also does occasional shifts giving advice at family law information centres that are funded by Legal Aid. She's also written a couple of murder mysteries and is currently working with an agent.

While she was still practicing law, Mutton started to think about how she would make the transition to being a writer. She took writing courses at her local community college on magazine and fiction writing. She got her finances in order. From the point that she felt she was ready, she says on her website, it only took her a month to close the door of her law office.

"The interviewing skills I gained as a lawyer have been really helpful. I can usually get the quotes I need within 15 minutes of being on the phone," she admits.

Some writers, like Kelley and Turow, can expect to make millions. Others who do not have the same success can still make a living of anywhere from $30,000 to $100,000 a year, depending on how much work they do and whether they include a component of corporate writing into their portfolio.

There's little overhead if you can take a small corner of your home to set up your office, and you can write off your expenses.

Those who have turned from law to writing and researching as a second career all have the same advice. Do not shut down your law firm on some romantic notion that you will suddenly become a bestseller. Get your skills in order; learn the basics of the writing business, and prepare a solid business plan before you make your move. Know what you are getting into, and try to secure a few contracts before you leave your legal practice. It is easier to grow your business from those than to start cold.

You can use your research and writing skills as well to work as an editor for legal publications and to write do-it-yourself law books.

Preparing booklets for advocacy groups on issues such as environmental law and personal business (writing wills, estate planning, buying property, landlord/tenancy issues and even getting a divorce are always in demand) is another outlet.

Other former lawyers turned writers become experts are offering legal advice through syndicated newspaper columns and magazines. You can also create blogs and websites or even serve as full-time editors of bar association newsletters and legal, business or accounting publications.

Aaron Street, publisher of www.Lawyerist.com, is a prime example of a former lawyer who is using his training to build a successful writing career. It is a leading site of legal marketing advice, as well as information on practice management and technology. He is also publisher of Lawyerist's sister publication, the legal humour site, www.BitterLawyer.com, proving that incorporating a legal background into a writing career doesn't have to be deadly serious or dull.

Chapter 8

Finding Work
That Really Matters

Jim Collins, one of the most influential management gurus of the past 30 years, captured the imagination of people seeking a fulfilling work life in 2000 when he wrote a book called "Good to Great."

In it he recounted the story of a professor he had who suggested that while his life was busy, it was not particularly fulfilling, rewarding or productive for him.

She asked him how he would change his behaviour if he learned one day that he had just inherited $20 million, but that he had only 10 more years to live. What would he stop doing in that situation?

Her question prompted Collins to write his first "stop-doing list" and he now compiles a new list each year.

"A great piece of art is composed not just of what is in the final piece, but equally important, what is not," Collins wrote. "It is the discipline to discard what does not fit – to cut out what might have already cost days or even years of effort – that distinguishes the truly exceptional artist and marks the ideal piece of work, be it a symphony, a novel, a painting, a company or, most important of all, a life."

As you prepare you "to-do" list to leave a law profession that no longer fulfills you, are you also preparing a "to-don't" list?

Restructuring your life and your career to one that makes you happy and satisfied is as much about deciding what parts of your old life no longer fit, as it is about deciding what parts you want to take with you.

This is not an easy process. We can liken it to cleaning out a basement or a shed. There are many things causing clutter within view, but it is often tough to decide what we can discard and what we should hold onto because we might need it later, or what we can't possibly put out with the trash because we love it and it has great memories for us.

You have made the decision to change and to search for work that really matters to you. One avenue worth serious consideration are the thousands of charity and non-profit organizations that need legal help to set up lasting foundations, to acquire grants to allow them to continue their good deeds, and to establish rules and practices of governance that permit them to evolve their roles and constitutions.

If you are thinking about moving far from the corporate world and into the realm of the non-profit world, it is a good idea to consider well in advance what really motivates you. Discard those things that do not, and fill up your new "to-do" list with work you believe will bring you great personal satisfaction.

The secret to re-inventing yourself after being a lawyer is to decide what you don't want to do anymore. Specify and enumerate all the things that hold you back from living the life you want, and doing the work you consider rewarding.

Look at the actions, behaviours and obligations that daily are sapping your energy and distracting your attention from where you really want to be in life. These are the things you need to avoid when you move forward.

Consider what your real motivations are as you strive to rekindle your enthusiasm for work and life.

Daniel Pink, a non-practicing lawyer and a former speech writer for Al Gore, recently spent two years studying the science of what motivates us. He published his results in what is now a bestseller: "Drive: The Surprising Truth About What Motivates Us."

He concludes that how we used to think about motivation really isn't valid. Instead, he identifies the complexities a job must offer to us to be motivating:

The first is the contingent motivators, the *extrinsic* rewards for doing a good job. We want to focus on simple, clear tasks. The trouble is that this focus restricts our creative thinking on complex problems.

To motivate ourselves to complete creative and complex work, we need *intrinsic* motivators, like autonomy, the ability to master a subject, and a clear sense of purpose.

Some companies have an inherent understanding of this. For example, Google offers their engineers one full paid day each week to work on any project they want.

But for many lawyers, both extrinsic and intrinsic motivators are lacking. Autonomy is pretty much out the door the minute you step inside any large corporation, whether it's a group of lawyers or accountants or engineers. Mastering new skills may not be a priority when you are practicing a special area of law. The goal instead is to get really good at what you do, stay abreast of any new developments, and then just keep doing it and doing it again.

There has to be a reason that being a lawyer is one of the few professions where there seems to be as many people advising you how to get out of it as to get in.

Lawyers looking for work that really makes a difference in this world often find themselves gazing in the director of non-profit organizations and foundations.

In the United States alone, there are more than 1.12 registered charities and foundations. In Canada, there are more than 86,000 registered charities in an industry worth up to $207 billion a year. There are more than 100,000 non-profit organizations.

This is a growing field as more and more social agencies move in to fill the gaps in essential needs to regions hard hit by recessions and unemployment and gaps in health care insurance.

Lawyers in turning from corporate to public interest work find themselves switching their focus from the privileged to the disadvantaged. Typical cases can find lawyers seeking medical benefits for AIDs patients or patients made ill from environmental issues. They are engaged in landlord-tenant disagreements or child visitation rights arguments.

Many public interest lawyers find themselves affiliated with organizations trying to change the laws to protect those who can no longer protect themselves: the elderly, the young, and the poor. Sometimes they have to advocate for tolerance for people from different races and religions, and sometimes for people with different lifestyles.

Often there is a teaching component when working with non-profits. Many lawyers set up workshops to help disadvantaged citizens learn more about their personal human and civil rights and how to secure essential documents they need.

Training is often needed for board members and staff on issues concerning the law and ethics.

Those setting up organizations to help people in need often need legal assistance to obtain their registered charity status. These groups often need help to present their books properly for audits or to conduct their good works on an international scale.

Staffing issues need legal advice, as do the procurement of formal agreements with donors and funders. Intellectual property may need protection, and sometimes patents must be filed.

Seeking something completely different that still makes use of the law skills you acquired? Consider Lawyers Without Borders, the international, non-profit organization started in 2000 and now operating worldwide from its central headquarters in Hartford, Connecticut, US.

Meanwhile, Lawyers Without Borders UK was founded in 2003, and is affiliated with the American-based organization.

To date, the countries who contribute the largest number of lawyer volunteers to Lawyers Without Borders field work are United States, Canada, the United Kingdom and Australia.

The goal of the group is to provide pro bono rule of law work. The group trains judges and lawyers to build up a judicial sector in developing nations. It also employs week-long intense training sessions in criminal law, trafficking in persons, inheritance and succession and gender based and domestic violence.

The organization's orientation is strictly neutral, like the Red Cross. LWOB's programming and models have been implemented throughout Africa (Liberia, Kenya, Ethiopia, Namibia, Cameroon, Tanzania, Mozambique, Rwanda and Uganda). Regions outside Africa where work has been conducted or is planned include: Kyrgyzstan, China, Cuba, Albania, and India.

If you want to volunteer for Lawyers Without Borders, go to their website at www.lawyerswithoutborders.org and click on the Attorneys Volunteer Now sign. It will lead you to the "Lawyer Intake Form" to be filled out and submit.

If you are interested in working in the non-profit sector, you can start by freeing up your schedule so you can get involved in just one community non-profit organization and assist pro-bono with their legal work.

After a few months, you will see more clearly the kind of work to be done and understand if this is something that really interests you. If you are interested in Lawyers Without Borders, you can likely volunteer for a program or two while still keeping your day job while you decide if this kind of work gives you the fulfillment you seek.

If you do decide to work for a foundation, remember there are many different kinds and you should take the time to find one that fits with what you want. Study the foundation's purposes and specific programs and take a good look at its working environment.

Find out if the foundation's board is an active group with lots of input, or a group of individuals serving primarily as a rubber stamp. Find out how closely the foundation is tied to a funding source, and how many sources it draws from.

Once you find a foundation that really interests you, start lobbying to get yourself onto its board. The more boards you serve on, the better you will be equipped to serve as a lawyer specializing in the operation or administration of the foundation.

Chapter 9

Start Your Own Business

There's a popular story about a lawyer deciding to make himself a cup of tea one Saturday afternoon when he noticed a leak coming from under his kitchen sink. He immediately called a local plumber.

The plumber took out a spanner from his tool bag, fiddled with the pipe for two minutes, then told the lawyer the problem was solved and handed him a bill for $300."

"Three hundred dollars for two minutes work? That's ridiculous," said the lawyer. "Even I don't charge that much and I'm a lawyer."

"No, I didn't charge that much when I was a lawyer either," replied the plumber.

While the story is amusing, it sets every lawyer's mind racing about the potential for them to be even more successful, and likely even happier, if they were running a business different from law.

Starting your own business whether through the purchase of a franchise or existing business, or starting from scratch, is an exciting option to consider when you want to quit being a lawyer for a living.

Cari Sommer, who practiced law for seven years before co-founding Urban Interns, a website that connects small business owners with job hunters seeking part-time work, said in a Wall Street Journal interview that legal training is never wasted even if the person with it doesn't work in the law.

"In the broadest terms, practicing law is about analyzing facts, solving problems, advocating a position, and communicating with clients and adversaries," she says. "I use these skills every day in my work as an entrepreneur."

The most important thing to consider when you are thinking about going into business is to keep your decision from being emotional. If you buy or start a business on a whim, you may be setting yourself up for even more grief and stress than you are currently bearing.

The annals of failed businesses are full of lawyers who thought they could run a restaurant because they ate in then a lot, or thought they could run a newspaper because they read one every day.

You know a lot about the law because you studied it. You need to amass a lot of knowledge about business and the kind of business you plan to open before you invest your hard-earned dollars into it.

Going into business as a means of getting out of lawyering is smart only when you see it as a way to make money, and in many case, more money than you are currently making. Otherwise, you would be better off taking up a new hobby.

You need to understand from the beginning exactly what the business is, what its product or service is, whether or not you can deliver it, who your competition is, and whether or not there is sufficient demand for this product or service to sustain your business.

If you do take the time to consider these points and build a thorough and logical business plan, you have an excellent chance of succeeding. That's because you already have great skills in negotiating contracts and making decisions on which course of action to take when there are many options. These are invaluable assets to the entrepreneur.

Remember that if you don't want to go into business for yourself, you still have options in the business world too. Your law skills make you a natural for moving into investment banking, real estate development and management consulting.

There are also many options to the notion of starting your own business. You can be a manufacturer owning a large plant with many employees or a solopreneur offering one skill that you personally provide. You can buy a bustling New York restaurant, or you can open a bed and breakfast in Canada's Cape Breton Island.

The skills you need will be the same, and in both cases you will be filling a niche, but the stress and resources needed to get started will vary immensely.

Ask yourself these five questions about any business venture you are considering:

- Can I describe this business in one paragraph (you need to have your vision pared down to a single focus).
- What product or service will I sell?
- Is there an unfilled need for this product or service?
- Is there an existing market for my product or service where demand exceeds supply?
- Can I compete with others who are currently offering my product or service?

The answers to these questions won't come off the top of your head. You will need to do your research and gather statistics. Gather both data and anecdotal evidence. Put your research skills to good use and dig up everything you can on your potential business opportunities and competition.

The more information you gather in the preliminary process, the better chance you have of making your business a success. You can do this while you are still working at the job you hate. In fact, as soon as you start the process, you will notice that you are less stressed by your job, because even doing the research sends your brain a single that you are contemplating your escape route.

Think about your potential customers and how you can meet their needs. Do you know who they are and how they think? Do you know where they live and their buying patterns? Will they be purchasing your product or service in person or on line?

Now put your legal brain in gear and gather research on some of the basics. Do you need a special licence or permit to operate the business you are considering? What are the laws that govern this business? Do you know how to register and name your business? Look into local ordinances, taxes, and even occupational health and safety requirements, depending on the nature of your business.

Consider a place for your business, and insurance for your business. If you are going to sell a product, consider sources for supplies of this product. Can you keep your own books, or should you involve an accountant in your business?

Then comes the really hard part, the finances. How much money are you willing to invest into any business that you will start? How much will it really take to get the business off the ground? (Consider renovations to a building, fixtures and equipment, initial inventory, licenses and permits, phones and computers, insurance, marketing tools, and unexpected expenses.) How long can you run the business before it turns a profit? Would it be wiser to stay with your day job in the early days of getting your business going until it starts to turn a good profit?

Some other considerations are whether or not there are seasonal trends in the business you are hoping to open and whether or how you will extend credit to your customers.

You may decide that buying a franchise is a better route to get started.

"For some people, it's buying themselves a job," is the way franchise lawyer Tony Wilson with Vancouver's Boughton Law firm puts it.

Wilson, author of "Buying A Franchise in Canada: Understanding and Negotiating Your Franchise Agreement," writes that doing extensive research yourself is still essential, regardless of whether you are buying a franchise or starting your own company.

He urges potential franchise buyers to consider whether or not the franchise they are looking at is reputable. Has it proven itself somewhere, and where? Would its success in the United States, for example, translate to Canada, or would cultural differences make it less popular?

Owning a franchise is not exactly the same thing as owning your own business.

"You never own the business, really. You're just renting it from somebody else," Wilson explains.

On the down side, franchises also frequently have high start up costs, such as construction for new locations, which can add hundreds of thousands of dollars to the price of the licence itself.

On the plus side, you get training in a system that has already been proven successful, you get access to a trade mark and brand advertising, and you can leverage joint purchasing power.

Psychologically, lawyers have the potential to turn themselves into very successful business people. A huge part of business is the ability to make decisions, and lawyers have to do that every time they approach a case. Another crucial talent is the ability to judge good people, and lawyers have an innate sense of that.

The skills you acquired as a lawyer will also help you in business. In fact, the law touches almost every aspect of operating a business from reviewing employment agreements to reviewing purchase contracts, checking for any liens or easements that restrict property use, and reviewing mortgage terms.

Your background also helps you in aspects of commercial law, copyrights, patents and trademarks, and employment and tort law.

As a lawyer, you also have an inherit understanding of the value of the billable hour and you know how to focus on your client, an essential component to business success too often lacking in new business owners.

Ultimately, while there are dozens of good options for you to consider in business, one of the simplest ways to make the transition is to take one aspect of your own skills that interests you, and decide to specialize in it within your own business.

For example, you could go into dispute resolution, hiring yourself out to corporations, non-profits, government agencies, hospitals, prisons, media organizations and unions to resolve disputes. You may need some additional mediation training, but you can acquire that while in your current job. One way to get started is to offer a training seminar to a local human resources association to help their members with dispute resolution. Who do you think they will end up calling when the problem gets to be more than they can handle?

You could become a legal instructor, acquiring a community college class as a basis of your business and branching out from there to textbooks and webinars and seminars. Many small businesses can't afford an on-staff lawyer, but they are eager to learn the basics, and then call their trusted consultant when the problem becomes too cumbersome.

Another business that attracts former practicing lawyers is becoming a lobbyist, where you draft and shepherd legislation through government channels on behalf of special interest groups.

Your familiarity with law firms make you a natural for providing services to them in your business, whether it is insurance, research, or even computer programs or systems.

You could also consider becoming a business valuation expert or an agent for artists or athletes, or join the growing field of career counsellors to lawyers.

The bottom line for lawyers looking for careers in business is to know themselves.

"A lawyer usually focuses on one issue and its resolution, whereas a business leader has to place the action taken on that issue in the broader context of its impact on the business," says lawyer turned entrepreneur David Stern.

If you have the right combination of personality and drive to become an entrepreneur, go for it. If you are allergic to risk and need weeks of research to make a decision, it may not be right for you. Only you know your true comfort zone.

Chapter 10

Changing How You Live To Make It Better: Voluntary Simplicity

Andrea Bocelli felt the songs in his soul from childhood. All he ever wanted to be was a musician.

Instead, to make a living, he took a law degree at the University of Pisa after he finished school. By the time he was 30 he was working full time as a lawyer, but his dream of making a life of music still burned within him.

He started moonlighting in a piano bar for fun and a little extra cash. About four years later he caught a break as a singer and his spellbinding voice now brings nations to their feet.

He didn't know when he left law that he could make a success of it. But he knew finally that his life, if it was to be full, had to have music. If that meant living with less to have more, so be it.

Today more and more people around the world are embracing a lifestyle of voluntary simplicity to achieve their true goals in life. They have decided that big bank balances, castle-size homes, and fast cars are not taking them where they want to go.

If you are unhappy as a lawyer, this option remains, to walk away and embrace a new lifestyle of scaling down and spending less to experience the wealth of freedom and independence.

The movement towards simple living is about 15 years old and it continues to grow in popularity. In the United Kingdom, for example, there is actually an annual "National Downshifting Week" campaign that encourages people to positively embrace living with less.

"The more money you spend, the more time you have to be out there earning it, and the less time you have to spend with the ones you love," says campaign creator Tracey Smith.

Reducing your possessions and the size of your home is all part of the simple living philosophy. In fact, one rapidly growing grassroots movement called "The 100 Thing Challenge" alls on people to whittle down their possessions to just 100 items. They believe this de-cluttering process will free people and also make it clear that they can live happily in smaller, mortgage-free buildings.

Hand-in-hand with the "buy less" aspect of the simple living philosophy is the "produce more" mantra. Many advocates start to grow their own food, embracing the joys of backyard gardening. Sometimes they add a few chickens as well to enhance their diet. Proponents of growing your own food embrace The 100 Mile Diet, meaning the food they eat should be locally produced, not trucked into their local market at great expense.

Simple living, in essence, is the opposite of our modern quest for affluence and career success. It is less about quantity and more about quality. It is less about growth and ore about the preservation of our planet, our cities and our traditions.

There is something about this movement that has sparked the imagination of many unhappy lawyers.

"Jack," for example, extolled readers to follow his blog, http://advenventuresinvoluntarysimplicity.blogspot.ca/ .

"Follow along as a former highly-paid lawyer gives up a life of material comfort and unencumbered excess, and embraces the beauty and freedom of simple happiness," he wrote as he embarked on his life-changing adventure.

Another blogster at www.earlyretirementextreme. com refers to his system of voluntary simplicity as "a way out for a young lawyer." Lawyers are encouraged to save 75 percent of their net income and invest it in income producing assets (bonds and dividend stocks) so they can retire at a young age.

Proponents of voluntary simplicity refer to it as living an examined life; in other words, living a life in which you have determined what is important for you and your immediate family, and discarding the rest. Such a life is incredibly inexpensive, and it's not stressful. The downside is that you lose some modern trappings that we have all grown used to, and there is a great deal of physical work involved.

Those who embrace it as a lifestyle say it hinges more on personal values than financial benefits. You have to ask yourself if the freedom of such a lifestyle is alluring enough to outweigh the work involved and the loss of some material and social goods.

Duane Elgin defines voluntary simplicity as living a life that is "outwardly simple and inwardly rich.... a deliberate choice to live with less in the belief that more life will be returned to us in the process." David Shi, who has written extensively about the movement, defines voluntary simplicity as "enlightened material restraint."

The rudimentary foundation of the movement, often called the quiet revolution, is a suspicion of luxuries, a reverence and respect for nature, a desire for self-sufficiency, a consideration of creativity and contemplation over possessions, and a sense of responsibility for the just use of the world's resources.

What it does not mean is a life of poverty or a renouncing of the advantages of science and technology. It is not for puritans or hippies, but rather a reasoned examination of the way our culture has come to view and accumulate possessions.

As Leonardo da Vinci said: "Simplicity is the ultimate sophistication."

It strives to answer the questions posed by Henry David Thoreau:" What is it to be born free and not to live free?" One of the original advocates of voluntary simplicity, Thoreau felt that people were becoming slaves of an economical tyrant and lamented that their days were filled with "work, work, work."

If your career as a lawyer keeps you a slave to the economics of your current lifestyle, should you consider throwing off the chains of debt and consumerism and embracing a completely different lifestyle?

If you are inherently unhappy, you should. Changing jobs or changing professions isn't going to fill the void you feel by having to dedicate every waking moment to earning money not just to sustain yourself and your family, but to buy "things."

You can change and get your life back again. And again, your training can help you.

Proponents of this economic lifestyle often need legal advice on how to preserve their resources and the environment, and initiate action against those they feel are not respectful of the good earth. They are also interested in preserving political and ethical economies, and often need a well-reasoned brief to make their point.

Your old colleagues may think you are losing it. But when they visit you and find you actually have time to live as opposed to consume, they may also want to join you.

As Thoreau put it: "There is no more fatal blunderer than he who consumes the greater part of his life getting his living."

You may feel that you blundered in life when you took up law. Don't make a bigger mistake by continuing to live a life you hate.

There are exit signs and maps for new fulfillment and prosperity in every direction you look. With courage and planning, you can reach the destination you desire.

Appendix

Other useful resources dealing with career changes for lawyers:

- *What Can You Do With a Law Degree? A Lawyer's Guide to Career Alternatives Inside, Outside & Around the Law* by Deborah Arron.
- *The Unhappy Lawyer* by Monica Parker.
- *Judgment Reversed: Alternative Careers for Lawyers* by Jeffrey Strausser.
- *The Lawyer's Career Change Handbook: More than 300 Things You Can Do With a Law Degree* by Hindi Greenberg.
- *JD Preferred: 400+ Things You Can do With a Law Degree (Other Than Practice Law)*, published by Federal Reports, Inc.
- *Alternative Careers for Lawyers* by Hillary Mantis.

List of transferable legal skills

The following legal skills identified on <u>Life After Law</u> are valued in non-traditional jobs for lawyers:

Ability to work independently	Communication
Analytical thinking	Conflict Resolution
Attention to detail	Counselling
Awareness of risk or liability	Creativity
Brainstorming	Decision making
Budgeting	Discipline

Dissemination of information
Entrepreneurial
Fact analysis
Identification of issues
Innovation
Interpersonal skills
Interpretation of documents
Learning
Management
Mediation
Multi-Tasking
Negotiation
Organizational skills
Persuasion
Presentation skills
Prioritization

Problem Solving
Professionalism
Project Management
Public Speaking
Research
Sales
Self-Direction
Strategizing
Stress Management
Supervisory
Synthesis of information
Teamwork
Time Management
Troubleshooting
Writing

www.ingramcontent.com/pod-product-compliance
Lightning Source LLC
Chambersburg PA
CBHW071120210326
41519CB00020B/6358